NAME:

# 14ER LOGBOOK

"**Travel** makes one modest.
You see what a tiny place
you occupy in the **World**."
–Gustave Flaubert

# FOURTEENER LOGBOOK

**DATE:** ☀ ⛅ ☁ ☂ ⛆ ⛈ ❄ 🌫 ☐Hot ☐Cold ☐Mild

| | |
|---|---|
| Start Date/Time: | End Date/Time: |
| Total Hike Time To Summit: | Total Distance Hiked: |
| Start Elevation: | End Elevation: |
| Total Elevation Conquered: | Did you Summit on Day 1?   Y / N |

## THE PEAK: ☆☆☆☆☆

Peak Name:

Range: _____  Elevation:

Lat/Lon:

City, State:

Peak Conditions:

Cell Phone Reception/Carrier:

☐First Visit   ☐Return Visit    Personal Rating: Easy / Intermediate / Difficult

14er Companions:

Route Taken:

Trail Features & Conditions:

Were there places to refill water?  Explain:

Did you stay the night along the way or back?  Details:

Notes for next time (shuttles, entrance fees, parking, routes, etc):

# NOTES / JOURNALING

# FOURTEENER LOGBOOK

**DATE:** ☀ ⛅ ☁ 🌧 ⛈ ❄ 🌫 ☐Hot ☐Cold ☐Mild

| | |
|---|---|
| Start Date/Time: | End Date/Time: |
| Total Hike Time To Summit: | Total Distance Hiked: |
| Start Elevation: | End Elevation: |
| Total Elevation Conquered: | Did you Summit on Day 1?  Y / N |

## THE PEAK: ☆☆☆☆☆

Peak Name:

Range: _____ Elevation:

Lat/Lon:

City, State:

Peak Conditions:

Cell Phone Reception/Carrier:

☐First Visit  ☐Return Visit    Personal Rating:  Easy / Intermediate / Difficult

14er Companions:

Route Taken:

Trail Features & Conditions:

Were there places to refill water?  Explain:

Did you stay the night along the way or back?  Details:

Notes for next time (shuttles, entrance fees, parking, routes, etc):

# NOTES / JOURNALING

# FOURTEENER LOGBOOK

**DATE:** ☼ ⛅ ☁ 🌤 ⛈ ❄ 🌫 ☐Hot ☐Cold ☐Mild

| | |
|---|---|
| Start Date/Time: | End Date/Time: |
| Total Hike Time To Summit: | Total Distance Hiked: |
| Start Elevation: | End Elevation: |
| Total Elevation Conquered: | Did you Summit on Day 1?   Y / N |

## THE PEAK:  ☆☆☆☆☆

Peak Name:

Range:            Elevation:

Lat/Lon:

City, State:

Peak Conditions:

Cell Phone Reception/Carrier:

☐First Visit   ☐Return Visit   Personal Rating:  Easy / Intermediate / Difficult

14er Companions:

Route Taken:

Trail Features & Conditions:

Were there places to refill water?  Explain:

Did you stay the night along the way or back?  Details:

Notes for next time (shuttles, entrance fees, parking, routes, etc):

# NOTES / JOURNALING

# FOURTEENER LOGBOOK

## DATE: ☀ ⛅ ☁ 🌦 ⛈ ❄ 🌫 ☐Hot ☐Cold ☐Mild

Start Date/Time: _____ End Date/Time: _____

Total Hike Time To Summit: _____ Total Distance Hiked: _____

Start Elevation: _____ End Elevation: _____

Total Elevation Conquered: _____ Did you Summit on Day 1?   Y / N

## THE PEAK: ☆ ☆ ☆ ☆ ☆

Peak Name: _____

Range: _____ Elevation: _____

Lat/Lon: _____

City, State: _____

Peak Conditions: _____

Cell Phone Reception/Carrier: _____

☐First Visit   ☐Return Visit     Personal Rating:  Easy / Intermediate / Difficult

14er Companions: _____

Route Taken: _____

Trail Features & Conditions: _____

Were there places to refill water?  Explain: _____

Did you stay the night along the way or back?  Details: _____

Notes for next time (shuttles, entrance fees, parking, routes, etc): _____

# NOTES / JOURNALING

# FOURTEENER LOGBOOK

**DATE:** ☼ ⛅ ☁ 🌥 🌦 ❄ 🌫 ☐Hot ☐Cold ☐Mild

Start Date/Time: _____ | End Date/Time: _____
Total Hike Time To Summit: _____ | Total Distance Hiked: _____
Start Elevation: _____ | End Elevation: _____
Total Elevation Conquered: _____ | Did you Summit on Day 1?   Y / N

## THE PEAK: ☆☆☆☆☆

Peak Name: _____

Range: _____ | Elevation: _____

Lat/Lon: _____

City, State: _____

Peak Conditions: _____

Cell Phone Reception/Carrier: _____

☐First Visit   ☐Return Visit      Personal Rating:  Easy / Intermediate / Difficult

14er Companions: _____

Route Taken: _____

Trail Features & Conditions: _____

Were there places to refill water?  Explain: _____

Did you stay the night along the way or back?  Details: _____

Notes for next time (shuttles, entrance fees, parking, routes, etc): _____

# NOTES / JOURNALING

# FOURTEENER LOGBOOK

**DATE:** ☼ ⛅ ☁ ☁ ⛈ ❄ 🌫 ☐Hot ☐Cold ☐Mild

Start Date/Time: ........................................ End Date/Time: ........................................

Total Hike Time To Summit: ..................... Total Distance Hiked: ...........................

Start Elevation: ...................................... End Elevation: .......................................

Total Elevation Conquered: ...................... Did you Summit on Day 1?   Y / N

## THE PEAK: ☆ ☆ ☆ ☆ ☆

Peak Name: ...............................................................................................................

Range: ..................................... Elevation: ............................

Lat/Lon: ...................................................................................................................

City, State: ..............................................................................................................

Peak Conditions: .....................................................................................................

Cell Phone Reception/Carrier: ................................................................................

☐First Visit   ☐Return Visit     Personal Rating:  Easy / Intermediate / Difficult

14er Companions: ....................................................................................................

Route Taken: ...........................................................................................................

Trail Features & Conditions: ...................................................................................

Were there places to refill water?  Explain: .........................................................

Did you stay the night along the way or back?  Details: .......................................

Notes for next time (shuttles, entrance fees, parking, routes, etc): ...................

# NOTES / JOURNALING

# FOURTEENER LOGBOOK

**DATE:** ☀ ⛅ ☁ 🌧 ⛈ ❄ 🌫 ☐Hot ☐Cold ☐Mild

Start Date/Time:_____ End Date/Time:_____

Total Hike Time To Summit:_____ Total Distance Hiked:_____

Start Elevation:_____ End Elevation:_____

Total Elevation Conquered:_____ Did you Summit on Day 1?   Y / N

## THE PEAK: ☆☆☆☆☆

Peak Name:_____

Range:_____ Elevation:_____

Lat/Lon:_____

City, State:_____

Peak Conditions:_____

Cell Phone Reception/Carrier:_____

☐First Visit  ☐Return Visit   Personal Rating:  Easy / Intermediate / Difficult

14er Companions:_____

Route Taken:_____

Trail Features & Conditions:_____

Were there places to refill water?  Explain:_____

Did you stay the night along the way or back?  Details:_____

Notes for next time (shuttles, entrance fees, parking, routes, etc):_____

# NOTES / JOURNALING

# FOURTEENER LOGBOOK

## DATE: ☼ ⛅ ☁ ☂ ⛈ ❄ 🌫 ☐Hot ☐Cold ☐Mild

Start Date/Time: _____    End Date/Time: _____

Total Hike Time To Summit: _____    Total Distance Hiked: _____

Start Elevation: _____    End Elevation: _____

Total Elevation Conquered: _____    Did you Summit on Day 1?  Y / N

## THE PEAK: ☆☆☆☆☆

Peak Name: _____

Range: _____    Elevation: _____

Lat/Lon: _____

City, State: _____

Peak Conditions: _____

Cell Phone Reception/Carrier: _____

☐First Visit  ☐Return Visit    Personal Rating:  Easy / Intermediate / Difficult

14er Companions: _____

Route Taken: _____

Trail Features & Conditions: _____

Were there places to refill water?  Explain: ____

Did you stay the night along the way or back?  Details: ____

Notes for next time (shuttles, entrance fees, parking, routes, etc): ____

# NOTES / JOURNALING

# FOURTEENER LOGBOOK

**DATE:** ☀ ⛅ ☁ 🌦 ⛈ ❄ 🌫 ☐Hot ☐Cold ☐Mild

Start Date/Time:_____ End Date/Time:_____

Total Hike Time To Summit:_____ Total Distance Hiked:_____

Start Elevation:_____ End Elevation:_____

Total Elevation Conquered:_____ Did you Summit on Day 1?  Y / N

## THE PEAK: ☆☆☆☆☆

Peak Name:_____

Range:_____ Elevation:_____

Lat/Lon:_____

City, State:_____

Peak Conditions:_____

Cell Phone Reception/Carrier:_____

☐First Visit  ☐Return Visit   Personal Rating: Easy / Intermediate / Difficult

14er Companions:_____

Route Taken:_____

Trail Features & Conditions:_____

Were there places to refill water?  Explain:_____

Did you stay the night along the way or back?  Details:_____

Notes for next time (shuttles, entrance fees, parking, routes, etc):_____

# NOTES / JOURNALING

# FOURTEENER LOGBOOK

**DATE:** ☀ ⛅ ☁ 🌧 ⛈ ❄ 🌫 ☐Hot ☐Cold ☐Mild

Start Date/Time:_____ End Date/Time:_____

Total Hike Time To Summit:_____ Total Distance Hiked:_____

Start Elevation:_____ End Elevation:_____

Total Elevation Conquered:_____ Did you Summit on Day 1?  Y / N

## THE PEAK: ☆☆☆☆☆

Peak Name:_____

Range:_____ Elevation:_____

Lat/Lon:_____

City, State:_____

Peak Conditions:_____

Cell Phone Reception/Carrier:_____

☐First Visit  ☐Return Visit    Personal Rating:  Easy / Intermediate / Difficult

14er Companions:_____

Route Taken:_____

Trail Features & Conditions:_____

Were there places to refill water?  Explain:_____

Did you stay the night along the way or back?  Details:_____

Notes for next time (shuttles, entrance fees, parking, routes, etc):_____

# NOTES / JOURNALING

# FOURTEENER LOGBOOK

**DATE:** ☀ ⛅ ☁ 🌧 ⛈ ❄ 🌫 ☐Hot ☐Cold ☐Mild

Start Date/Time:_____ End Date/Time:_____

Total Hike Time To Summit:_____ Total Distance Hiked:_____

Start Elevation:_____ End Elevation:_____

Total Elevation Conquered:_____ Did you Summit on Day 1?  Y / N

## THE PEAK: ☆☆☆☆☆

Peak Name:_____

Range:_____ Elevation:_____

Lat/Lon:_____

City, State:_____

Peak Conditions:_____

Cell Phone Reception/Carrier:_____

☐First Visit  ☐Return Visit    Personal Rating: Easy / Intermediate / Difficult

14er Companions:_____

Route Taken:_____

Trail Features & Conditions:_____

Were there places to refill water?  Explain:_____

Did you stay the night along the way or back?  Details:_____

Notes for next time (shuttles, entrance fees, parking, routes, etc):_____

# NOTES / JOURNALING

# FOURTEENER LOGBOOK

**DATE:** ☀ ⛅ ☁ 🌧 ⛈ ❄ 🌫 ☐Hot ☐Cold ☐Mild

Start Date/Time: ...............................    End Date/Time: ...............................

Total Hike Time To Summit: ...............    Total Distance Hiked: ...................

Start Elevation: ................................    End Elevation: ................................

Total Elevation Conquered: ...............    Did you Summit on Day 1?  Y / N

## THE PEAK:    ☆ ☆ ☆ ☆ ☆

Peak Name: ....................................................................

Range: ...............................    Elevation: ...............................

Lat/Lon: ........................................................................

City, State: .....................................................................

Peak Conditions: .............................................................

Cell Phone Reception/Carrier: ..........................................

☐First Visit    ☐Return Visit    Personal Rating:  Easy / Intermediate / Difficult

14er Companions: ............................................................

Route Taken: ...................................................................

Trail Features & Conditions: .............................................

Were there places to refill water?  Explain: .....................

Did you stay the night along the way or back?  Details: .....

Notes for next time (shuttles, entrance fees, parking, routes, etc): .....

# NOTES / JOURNALING

# FOURTEENER LOGBOOK

## DATE: ☼ ⛅ ☁ ☂ ⚡ ❄ ☁ □Hot □Cold □Mild

Start Date/Time: _____ | End Date/Time: _____

Total Hike Time To Summit: _____ | Total Distance Hiked: _____

Start Elevation: _____ | End Elevation: _____

Total Elevation Conquered: _____ | Did you Summit on Day 1?  Y / N

## THE PEAK: ☆☆☆☆☆

Peak Name: _____

Range: _____ | Elevation: _____

Lat/Lon: _____

City, State: _____

Peak Conditions: _____

Cell Phone Reception/Carrier: _____

□First Visit   □Return Visit   Personal Rating: Easy / Intermediate / Difficult

14er Companions: _____

Route Taken: _____

Trail Features & Conditions: _____

Were there places to refill water?  Explain: _____

Did you stay the night along the way or back?  Details: _____

Notes for next time (shuttles, entrance fees, parking, routes, etc): _____

# NOTES / JOURNALING

# FOURTEENER LOGBOOK

**DATE:** ☼ ⛅ ☁ ☂ ⛈ ❄ 🌫 ☐Hot ☐Cold ☐Mild

Start Date/Time:................................. End Date/Time:.................................

Total Hike Time To Summit:................. Total Distance Hiked:.........................

Start Elevation:................................... End Elevation:...................................

Total Elevation Conquered:................. Did you Summit on Day 1?   Y / N

## THE PEAK: ☆☆☆☆☆

Peak Name:.............................................................................................

Range:.................................... Elevation:.................................

Lat/Lon:.................................................................................................

City, State:.............................................................................................

Peak Conditions:....................................................................................

Cell Phone Reception/Carrier:...............................................................

☐First Visit   ☐Return Visit   Personal Rating:  Easy / Intermediate / Difficult

14er Companions:...................................................................................

Route Taken:...........................................................................................

Trail Features & Conditions:...................................................................

Were there places to refill water?  Explain:...........................................

Did you stay the night along the way or back?  Details:.........................

Notes for next time (shuttles, entrance fees, parking, routes, etc):.......

# NOTES / JOURNALING

# FOURTEENER LOGBOOK

**DATE:** ☀ ⛅ ☁ 🌧 ⛈ ❄ 🌫 ☐Hot ☐Cold ☐Mild

Start Date/Time:............................ End Date/Time:...........................

Total Hike Time To Summit:............ Total Distance Hiked:...................

Start Elevation:............................. End Elevation:...........................

Total Elevation Conquered:............. Did you Summit on Day 1?   Y / N

## THE PEAK: ☆☆☆☆☆

Peak Name:....................................................................

Range:........................................ Elevation:.........................

Lat/Lon:.........................................................................

City, State:.....................................................................

Peak Conditions:..............................................................

Cell Phone Reception/Carrier:..............................................

☐First Visit   ☐Return Visit     Personal Rating:  Easy / Intermediate / Difficult

14er Companions:.............................................................

Route Taken:...................................................................

Trail Features & Conditions:................................................

Were there places to refill water?  Explain:...........................

Did you stay the night along the way or back?  Details:.............

Notes for next time (shuttles, entrance fees, parking, routes, etc):.....

# NOTES / JOURNALING

# FOURTEENER LOGBOOK

**DATE:** ☀ ⛅ ☁ ☂ ⚡ ❄ 🌫 ☐Hot ☐Cold ☐Mild

Start Date/Time:................................... End Date/Time:...................

Total Hike Time To Summit:................. Total Distance Hiked:...........

Start Elevation:.................................... End Elevation:.....................

Total Elevation Conquered:................. Did you Summit on Day 1?   Y / N

## THE PEAK:    ☆ ☆ ☆ ☆ ☆

Peak Name:...............................................................................

Range:....................................... Elevation:...............................

Lat/Lon:..................................................................................

City, State:.............................................................................

Peak Conditions:......................................................................

Cell Phone Reception/Carrier:................................................

☐First Visit   ☐Return Visit     Personal Rating:  Easy / Intermediate / Difficult

14er Companions:...................................................................

Route Taken:............................................................................

Trail Features & Conditions:....................................................

Were there places to refill water?  Explain:...........................

Did you stay the night along the way or back?  Details:...........

Notes for next time (shuttles, entrance fees, parking, routes, etc):...........

# NOTES / JOURNALING

# FOURTEENER LOGBOOK

## DATE: ☼ ⛅ ☁ ☁ ⛆ ⛈ ❄ 🌫 □Hot □Cold □Mild

| | |
|---|---|
| Start Date/Time: | End Date/Time: |
| Total Hike Time To Summit: | Total Distance Hiked: |
| Start Elevation: | End Elevation: |
| Total Elevation Conquered: | Did you Summit on Day 1?   Y / N |

## THE PEAK: ☆ ☆ ☆ ☆ ☆

Peak Name:

Range: Elevation:

Lat/Lon:

City, State:

Peak Conditions:

Cell Phone Reception/Carrier:

□First Visit   □Return Visit    Personal Rating: Easy / Intermediate / Difficult

14er Companions:

Route Taken:

Trail Features & Conditions:

Were there places to refill water?  Explain:

Did you stay the night along the way or back?  Details:

Notes for next time (shuttles, entrance fees, parking, routes, etc):

# NOTES / JOURNALING

# FOURTEENER LOGBOOK

**DATE:** ☀ ⛅ ☁ 🌧 ⛈ ❄ 🌫 ☐Hot ☐Cold ☐Mild

Start Date/Time: ............................... End Date/Time: ...............................

Total Hike Time To Summit: ............... Total Distance Hiked: .....................

Start Elevation: ................................ End Elevation: ................................

Total Elevation Conquered: ............... Did you Summit on Day 1?   Y / N

## THE PEAK:    ☆ ☆ ☆ ☆ ☆

Peak Name: ...............................................................................................

Range: ..................................... Elevation: ...............................

Lat/Lon: ...................................................................................................

City, State: ...............................................................................................

Peak Conditions: ......................................................................................

Cell Phone Reception/Carrier: ...............................................................

☐First Visit   ☐Return Visit     Personal Rating: Easy / Intermediate / Difficult

14er Companions: .....................................................................................

Route Taken: .............................................................................................

Trail Features & Conditions: ...................................................................

Were there places to refill water?  Explain: .........................................

Did you stay the night along the way or back?  Details: .....................

Notes for next time (shuttles, entrance fees, parking, routes, etc): .....

# NOTES / JOURNALING

# FOURTEENER LOGBOOK

**DATE:** ☼ ⛅ ☁ 🌧 ⚡ ❄ 🌬 ☐Hot ☐Cold ☐Mild

Start Date/Time:................................... End Date/Time:...................................

Total Hike Time To Summit:............... Total Distance Hiked:.........................

Start Elevation:................................... End Elevation:......................................

Total Elevation Conquered:............... Did you Summit on Day 1?   Y / N

## THE PEAK:                    ☆☆☆☆☆

Peak Name:................................................................................

Range:.................................... Elevation:...........................

Lat/Lon:.................................................................................

City, State:............................................................................

Peak Conditions:...................................................................

Cell Phone Reception/Carrier:...........................................

☐First Visit   ☐Return Visit     Personal Rating:  Easy / Intermediate / Difficult

14er Companions:................................................................

Route Taken:.........................................................................

Trail Features & Conditions:...............................................

Were there places to refill water?  Explain:...................

Did you stay the night along the way or back?  Details:..........

Notes for next time (shuttles, entrance fees, parking, routes, etc):..........

# NOTES / JOURNALING

# FOURTEENER LOGBOOK

**DATE:** ☼ ⛅ ☁ 🌧 ⛈ ❄ 🌬 ☐Hot ☐Cold ☐Mild

Start Date/Time: ................................. End Date/Time: ...................................

Total Hike Time To Summit: ..................... Total Distance Hiked: ...........................

Start Elevation: ................................ End Elevation: .................................

Total Elevation Conquered: ..................... Did you Summit on Day 1?   Y / N

## THE PEAK: ☆ ☆ ☆ ☆ ☆

Peak Name: ...........................................................................................

Range: ........................................... Elevation: ....................................

Lat/Lon: .............................................................................................

City, State: .........................................................................................

Peak Conditions: ....................................................................................

Cell Phone Reception/Carrier: .......................................................................

☐First Visit   ☐Return Visit     Personal Rating:  Easy / Intermediate / Difficult

14er Companions: ...................................................................................

Route Taken: .......................................................................................

Trail Features & Conditions: ......................................................................

Were there places to refill water?  Explain: ......................................................

Did you stay the night along the way or back?  Details: ..........................................

Notes for next time (shuttles, entrance fees, parking, routes, etc): .............................

# NOTES / JOURNALING

# FOURTEENER LOGBOOK

**DATE:** ☀ ⛅ ☁ 🌦 ⛈ ❄ 🌫 ☐Hot ☐Cold ☐Mild

| | |
|---|---|
| Start Date/Time: | End Date/Time: |
| Total Hike Time To Summit: | Total Distance Hiked: |
| Start Elevation: | End Elevation: |
| Total Elevation Conquered: | Did you Summit on Day 1?   Y / N |

## THE PEAK:  ☆ ☆ ☆ ☆ ☆

Peak Name:

Range: _____ Elevation:

Lat/Lon:

City, State:

Peak Conditions:

Cell Phone Reception/Carrier:

☐First Visit   ☐Return Visit     Personal Rating:  Easy / Intermediate / Difficult

14er Companions:

Route Taken:

Trail Features & Conditions:

Were there places to refill water?  Explain:

Did you stay the night along the way or back?  Details:

Notes for next time (shuttles, entrance fees, parking, routes, etc):

# NOTES / JOURNALING

# FOURTEENER LOGBOOK

## DATE: ☼ ⛅ ☁ 🌧 ⛈ ❄ 🌬 ☐Hot ☐Cold ☐Mild

Start Date/Time: _____ End Date/Time: _____

Total Hike Time To Summit: _____ Total Distance Hiked: _____

Start Elevation: _____ End Elevation: _____

Total Elevation Conquered: _____ Did you Summit on Day 1?   Y / N

## THE PEAK: ☆☆☆☆☆

Peak Name: _____

Range: _____ Elevation: _____

Lat/Lon: _____

City, State: _____

Peak Conditions: _____

Cell Phone Reception/Carrier: _____

☐First Visit   ☐Return Visit     Personal Rating:  Easy / Intermediate / Difficult

14er Companions: _____

Route Taken: _____

Trail Features & Conditions: _____

Were there places to refill water?  Explain: _____

Did you stay the night along the way or back?  Details: _____

Notes for next time (shuttles, entrance fees, parking, routes, etc): _____

# NOTES / JOURNALING

# FOURTEENER LOGBOOK

**DATE:** ☼ ⛅ ☁ ☂ ⚡ ❄ 🌬 ☐Hot ☐Cold ☐Mild

| | |
|---|---|
| Start Date/Time: | End Date/Time: |
| Total Hike Time To Summit: | Total Distance Hiked: |
| Start Elevation: | End Elevation: |
| Total Elevation Conquered: | Did you Summit on Day 1?   Y / N |

## THE PEAK: ☆☆☆☆☆

Peak Name:

Range: _____  Elevation:

Lat/Lon:

City, State:

Peak Conditions:

Cell Phone Reception/Carrier:

☐First Visit   ☐Return Visit   Personal Rating:  Easy / Intermediate / Difficult

14er Companions:

Route Taken:

Trail Features & Conditions:

Were there places to refill water?  Explain:

Did you stay the night along the way or back?  Details:

Notes for next time (shuttles, entrance fees, parking, routes, etc):

# NOTES / JOURNALING

# FOURTEENER LOGBOOK

## DATE: ☼ ⛅ ☁ ☂ ⚡ ❄ 🌫 ☐Hot ☐Cold ☐Mild

Start Date/Time:_____ End Date/Time:_____

Total Hike Time To Summit:_____ Total Distance Hiked:_____

Start Elevation:_____ End Elevation:_____

Total Elevation Conquered:_____ Did you Summit on Day 1?   Y / N

## THE PEAK: ☆☆☆☆☆

Peak Name:_____

Range:_____ Elevation:_____

Lat/Lon:_____

City, State:_____

Peak Conditions:_____

Cell Phone Reception/Carrier:_____

☐First Visit   ☐Return Visit    Personal Rating:  Easy / Intermediate / Difficult

14er Companions:_____

Route Taken:_____

Trail Features & Conditions:_____

Were there places to refill water?  Explain:_____

Did you stay the night along the way or back?  Details:_____

Notes for next time (shuttles, entrance fees, parking, routes, etc):_____

# NOTES / JOURNALING

# FOURTEENER LOGBOOK

**DATE:** ☼ ⛅ ☁ ☂ ⛈ ❄ 🌫 ☐Hot ☐Cold ☐Mild

| | |
|---|---|
| Start Date/Time: | End Date/Time: |
| Total Hike Time To Summit: | Total Distance Hiked: |
| Start Elevation: | End Elevation: |
| Total Elevation Conquered: | Did you Summit on Day 1?   Y / N |

## THE PEAK: ☆☆☆☆☆

Peak Name:

Range: ............................................ Elevation:

Lat/Lon:

City, State:

Peak Conditions:

Cell Phone Reception/Carrier:

☐First Visit   ☐Return Visit     Personal Rating: Easy / Intermediate / Difficult

14er Companions:

Route Taken:

Trail Features & Conditions:

Were there places to refill water?  Explain:

Did you stay the night along the way or back?  Details:

Notes for next time (shuttles, entrance fees, parking, routes, etc):

# NOTES / JOURNALING

# FOURTEENER LOGBOOK

**DATE:** ☼ ⛅ ☁ 🌧 ⛈ ❄ 🌫 ☐Hot ☐Cold ☐Mild

Start Date/Time: _____ End Date/Time: _____

Total Hike Time To Summit: _____ Total Distance Hiked: _____

Start Elevation: _____ End Elevation: _____

Total Elevation Conquered: _____ Did you Summit on Day 1?   Y / N

## THE PEAK: ☆☆☆☆☆

Peak Name: _____

Range: _____ Elevation: _____

Lat/Lon: _____

City, State: _____

Peak Conditions: _____

Cell Phone Reception/Carrier: _____

☐First Visit   ☐Return Visit    Personal Rating:  Easy / Intermediate / Difficult

14er Companions: _____

Route Taken: _____

Trail Features & Conditions: _____

Were there places to refill water?  Explain: _____

Did you stay the night along the way or back?  Details: _____

Notes for next time (shuttles, entrance fees, parking, routes, etc): _____

# FOURTEENER LOGBOOK

**DATE:** ☀ ⛅ ☁ ☂ ⚡ ❄ 🌫 ☐Hot ☐Cold ☐Mild

Start Date/Time: _____ End Date/Time: _____

Total Hike Time To Summit: _____ Total Distance Hiked: _____

Start Elevation: _____ End Elevation: _____

Total Elevation Conquered: _____ Did you Summit on Day 1?  Y / N

**THE PEAK:** ☆ ☆ ☆ ☆ ☆

Peak Name: _____

Range: _____ Elevation: _____

Lat/Lon: _____

City, State: _____

Peak Conditions: _____

Cell Phone Reception/Carrier: _____

☐First Visit   ☐Return Visit     Personal Rating:  Easy / Intermediate / Difficult

14er Companions: _____

Route Taken: _____

Trail Features & Conditions: _____

Were there places to refill water?  Explain: _____

Did you stay the night along the way or back?  Details: _____

Notes for next time (shuttles, entrance fees, parking, routes, etc): _____

# NOTES / JOURNALING

# FOURTEENER LOGBOOK

**DATE:** ☀ ⛅ ☁ 🌧 ⛈ ❄ 🌫 ☐Hot ☐Cold ☐Mild

Start Date/Time: _____ End Date/Time: _____

Total Hike Time To Summit: _____ Total Distance Hiked: _____

Start Elevation: _____ End Elevation: _____

Total Elevation Conquered: _____ Did you Summit on Day 1? Y / N

## THE PEAK: ☆☆☆☆☆

Peak Name: _____

Range: _____ Elevation: _____

Lat/Lon: _____

City, State: _____

Peak Conditions: _____

Cell Phone Reception/Carrier: _____

☐First Visit  ☐Return Visit    Personal Rating: Easy / Intermediate / Difficult

14er Companions: _____

Route Taken: _____

Trail Features & Conditions: _____

Were there places to refill water? Explain: _____

Did you stay the night along the way or back? Details: _____

Notes for next time (shuttles, entrance fees, parking, routes, etc): _____

# NOTES / JOURNALING

# FOURTEENER LOGBOOK

**DATE:** ☼ ⛅ ☁ ☁ 🌦 ⛈ ❄ ☔  ☐Hot  ☐Cold  ☐Mild

Start Date/Time:_____  End Date/Time:_____

Total Hike Time To Summit:_____  Total Distance Hiked:_____

Start Elevation:_____  End Elevation:_____

Total Elevation Conquered:_____  Did you Summit on Day 1?  Y / N

## THE PEAK: ☆☆☆☆☆

Peak Name:_____

Range:_____  Elevation:_____

Lat/Lon:_____

City, State:_____

Peak Conditions:_____

Cell Phone Reception/Carrier:_____

☐First Visit   ☐Return Visit   Personal Rating:  Easy / Intermediate / Difficult

14er Companions:_____

Route Taken:_____

Trail Features & Conditions:_____

Were there places to refill water?  Explain:_____

Did you stay the night along the way or back?  Details:_____

Notes for next time (shuttles, entrance fees, parking, routes, etc):_____

# NOTES / JOURNALING

# FOURTEENER LOGBOOK

**DATE:** ☀ ⛅ ☁ 🌧 ⛈ ❄ 🌬 □Hot □Cold □Mild

Start Date/Time:_____ | End Date/Time:_____
Total Hike Time To Summit:_____ | Total Distance Hiked:_____
Start Elevation:_____ | End Elevation:_____
Total Elevation Conquered:_____ | Did you Summit on Day 1?  Y / N

## THE PEAK: ☆☆☆☆☆

Peak Name:_____

Range:_____  Elevation:_____

Lat/Lon:_____

City, State:_____

Peak Conditions:_____

Cell Phone Reception/Carrier:_____

□First Visit   □Return Visit   Personal Rating:  Easy / Intermediate / Difficult

14er Companions:_____

Route Taken:_____

Trail Features & Conditions:_____

Were there places to refill water?  Explain:_____

Did you stay the night along the way or back?  Details:_____

Notes for next time (shuttles, entrance fees, parking, routes, etc):_____

# NOTES / JOURNALING

# FOURTEENER LOGBOOK

**DATE:** ☀ ⛅ ☁ ☂ ⚡ ❄ ☁ ☐Hot ☐Cold ☐Mild

Start Date/Time:............................ End Date/Time:............................

Total Hike Time To Summit:............ Total Distance Hiked:....................

Start Elevation:............................. End Elevation:.............................

Total Elevation Conquered:............ Did you Summit on Day 1?   Y / N

## THE PEAK: ☆☆☆☆☆

Peak Name:...................................................................................

Range:...................................... Elevation:..................................

Lat/Lon:........................................................................................

City, State:...................................................................................

Peak Conditions:...........................................................................

Cell Phone Reception/Carrier:.......................................................

☐First Visit   ☐Return Visit     Personal Rating:  Easy / Intermediate / Difficult

14er Companions:.........................................................................

Route Taken:................................................................................

Trail Features & Conditions:..........................................................

Were there places to refill water?  Explain:...................................

Did you stay the night along the way or back?  Details:...................

Notes for next time (shuttles, entrance fees, parking, routes, etc):...

# NOTES / JOURNALING

# FOURTEENER LOGBOOK

**DATE:** ☀ ⛅ ☁ ☁ 🌧 ⛈ ❄ 🌫 ☐Hot ☐Cold ☐Mild

Start Date/Time: _____ End Date/Time: _____

Total Hike Time To Summit: _____ Total Distance Hiked: _____

Start Elevation: _____ End Elevation: _____

Total Elevation Conquered: _____ Did you Summit on Day 1?   Y / N

## THE PEAK:  ☆☆☆☆☆

Peak Name: _____

Range: _____ Elevation: _____

Lat/Lon: _____

City, State: _____

Peak Conditions: _____

Cell Phone Reception/Carrier: _____

☐First Visit   ☐Return Visit   Personal Rating: Easy / Intermediate / Difficult

14er Companions: _____

Route Taken: _____

Trail Features & Conditions: _____

Were there places to refill water?  Explain: _____

Did you stay the night along the way or back?  Details: _____

Notes for next time (shuttles, entrance fees, parking, routes, etc): _____

# NOTES / JOURNALING

# FOURTEENER LOGBOOK

**DATE:** ☼ ⛅ ☁ ☁ 🌧 ⛈ ❄ 🌬 ☐Hot ☐Cold ☐Mild

Start Date/Time: _____ End Date/Time: _____

Total Hike Time To Summit: _____ Total Distance Hiked: _____

Start Elevation: _____ End Elevation: _____

Total Elevation Conquered: _____ Did you Summit on Day 1?  Y / N

## THE PEAK: ☆ ☆ ☆ ☆ ☆

Peak Name: _____

Range: _____ Elevation: _____

Lat/Lon: _____

City, State: _____

Peak Conditions: _____

Cell Phone Reception/Carrier: _____

☐First Visit  ☐Return Visit  Personal Rating:  Easy / Intermediate / Difficult

14er Companions: _____

Route Taken: _____

Trail Features & Conditions: _____

Were there places to refill water?  Explain: _____

Did you stay the night along the way or back?  Details: _____

Notes for next time (shuttles, entrance fees, parking, routes, etc): _____

# NOTES / JOURNALING

# FOURTEENER LOGBOOK

**DATE:** ☼ ⛅ ☁ ☂ ⚡ ❄ ☁ ☐Hot ☐Cold ☐Mild

| | |
|---|---|
| Start Date/Time: | End Date/Time: |
| Total Hike Time To Summit: | Total Distance Hiked: |
| Start Elevation: | End Elevation: |
| Total Elevation Conquered: | Did you Summit on Day 1?  Y / N |

## THE PEAK: ☆☆☆☆☆

Peak Name:

Range:      Elevation:

Lat/Lon:

City, State:

Peak Conditions:

Cell Phone Reception/Carrier:

☐First Visit   ☐Return Visit    Personal Rating:  Easy / Intermediate / Difficult

14er Companions:

Route Taken:

Trail Features & Conditions:

Were there places to refill water?  Explain:

Did you stay the night along the way or back?  Details:

Notes for next time (shuttles, entrance fees, parking, routes, etc):

# NOTES / JOURNALING

# FOURTEENER LOGBOOK

**DATE:** ☀ ⛅ ☁ 🌧 ⛈ ❄ 🌫 ☐Hot ☐Cold ☐Mild

Start Date/Time:_____ End Date/Time:_____

Total Hike Time To Summit:_____ Total Distance Hiked:_____

Start Elevation:_____ End Elevation:_____

Total Elevation Conquered:_____ Did you Summit on Day 1?  Y / N

## THE PEAK:  ☆☆☆☆☆

Peak Name:_____

Range:_____ Elevation:_____

Lat/Lon:_____

City, State:_____

Peak Conditions:_____

Cell Phone Reception/Carrier:_____

☐First Visit   ☐Return Visit     Personal Rating:  Easy / Intermediate / Difficult

14er Companions:_____

Route Taken:_____

Trail Features & Conditions:_____

Were there places to refill water?  Explain:_____

Did you stay the night along the way or back?  Details:_____

Notes for next time (shuttles, entrance fees, parking, routes, etc):____

# NOTES / JOURNALING

# FOURTEENER LOGBOOK

**DATE:** ☼ ⛅ ☁ ☂ ⚡ ❄ 🌫 ☐Hot ☐Cold ☐Mild

Start Date/Time:_____ End Date/Time:_____

Total Hike Time To Summit:_____ Total Distance Hiked:_____

Start Elevation:_____ End Elevation:_____

Total Elevation Conquered:_____ Did you Summit on Day 1?   Y / N

## THE PEAK: ☆☆☆☆☆

Peak Name:_____

Range:_____ Elevation:_____

Lat/Lon:_____

City, State:_____

Peak Conditions:_____

Cell Phone Reception/Carrier:_____

☐First Visit   ☐Return Visit     Personal Rating:  Easy / Intermediate / Difficult

14er Companions:_____

Route Taken:_____

Trail Features & Conditions:_____

Were there places to refill water?  Explain:_____

Did you stay the night along the way or back?  Details:_____

Notes for next time (shuttles, entrance fees, parking, routes, etc):_____

# NOTES / JOURNALING

# FOURTEENER LOGBOOK

**DATE:** ☀ ⛅ ☁ ☁ 🌧 ⛈ ❄ 🌬 ☐Hot ☐Cold ☐Mild

Start Date/Time: _____ End Date/Time: _____

Total Hike Time To Summit: _____ Total Distance Hiked: _____

Start Elevation: _____ End Elevation: _____

Total Elevation Conquered: _____ Did you Summit on Day 1?  Y / N

## THE PEAK: ☆ ☆ ☆ ☆ ☆

Peak Name: _____

Range: _____ Elevation: _____

Lat/Lon: _____

City, State: _____

Peak Conditions: _____

Cell Phone Reception/Carrier: _____

☐First Visit  ☐Return Visit   Personal Rating:  Easy / Intermediate / Difficult

14er Companions: _____

Route Taken: _____

Trail Features & Conditions: _____

Were there places to refill water?  Explain: _____

Did you stay the night along the way or back?  Details: _____

Notes for next time (shuttles, entrance fees, parking, routes, etc): _____

# NOTES / JOURNALING

# FOURTEENER LOGBOOK

**DATE:** ☀ ⛅ ☁ 🌧 ⛈ ❄ 🌫 ☐Hot ☐Cold ☐Mild

| | |
|---|---|
| Start Date/Time: | End Date/Time: |
| Total Hike Time To Summit: | Total Distance Hiked: |
| Start Elevation: | End Elevation: |
| Total Elevation Conquered: | Did you Summit on Day 1?  Y / N |

## THE PEAK: ☆☆☆☆☆

Peak Name:

Range: _____ Elevation:

Lat/Lon:

City, State:

Peak Conditions:

Cell Phone Reception/Carrier:

☐First Visit   ☐Return Visit    Personal Rating:  Easy / Intermediate / Difficult

14er Companions:

Route Taken:

Trail Features & Conditions:

Were there places to refill water?  Explain:

Did you stay the night along the way or back?  Details:

Notes for next time (shuttles, entrance fees, parking, routes, etc):

# NOTES / JOURNALING

# FOURTEENER LOGBOOK

**DATE:** ☀ ⛅ ☁ 🌧 ⛈ ❄ 🌫 ☐Hot ☐Cold ☐Mild

| | |
|---|---|
| Start Date/Time: | End Date/Time: |
| Total Hike Time To Summit: | Total Distance Hiked: |
| Start Elevation: | End Elevation: |
| Total Elevation Conquered: | Did you Summit on Day 1?  Y / N |

## THE PEAK: ☆☆☆☆☆

Peak Name:

| | |
|---|---|
| Range: | Elevation: |

Lat/Lon:

City, State:

Peak Conditions:

Cell Phone Reception/Carrier:

☐First Visit   ☐Return Visit      Personal Rating: Easy / Intermediate / Difficult

14er Companions:

Route Taken:

Trail Features & Conditions:

Were there places to refill water? Explain:

Did you stay the night along the way or back? Details:

Notes for next time (shuttles, entrance fees, parking, routes, etc):

# NOTES / JOURNALING

# FOURTEENER LOGBOOK

**DATE:** ☼ ⛅ ☁ ☁ 🌧 ⛈ ❄ 🌫 ☐Hot ☐Cold ☐Mild

Start Date/Time: _____ End Date/Time: _____

Total Hike Time To Summit: _____ Total Distance Hiked: _____

Start Elevation: _____ End Elevation: _____

Total Elevation Conquered: _____ Did you Summit on Day 1?   Y / N

## THE PEAK: ☆☆☆☆☆

Peak Name: _____

Range: _____ Elevation: _____

Lat/Lon: _____

City, State: _____

Peak Conditions: _____

Cell Phone Reception/Carrier: _____

☐First Visit   ☐Return Visit     Personal Rating:  Easy / Intermediate / Difficult

14er Companions: _____

Route Taken: _____

Trail Features & Conditions: _____

Were there places to refill water?  Explain: _____

Did you stay the night along the way or back?  Details: _____

Notes for next time (shuttles, entrance fees, parking, routes, etc): _____

# NOTES / JOURNALING

# FOURTEENER LOGBOOK

**DATE:** ☀ ⛅ ☁ 🌧 ⛈ ❄ 🌫 ☐Hot ☐Cold ☐Mild

Start Date/Time:_____ End Date/Time:_____

Total Hike Time To Summit:_____ Total Distance Hiked:_____

Start Elevation:_____ End Elevation:_____

Total Elevation Conquered:_____ Did you Summit on Day 1?   Y / N

## THE PEAK: ☆ ☆ ☆ ☆ ☆

Peak Name:_____

Range:_____ Elevation:_____

Lat/Lon:_____

City, State:_____

Peak Conditions:_____

Cell Phone Reception/Carrier:_____

☐First Visit   ☐Return Visit   Personal Rating:  Easy / Intermediate / Difficult

14er Companions:_____

Route Taken:_____

Trail Features & Conditions:_____

Were there places to refill water?  Explain:_____

Did you stay the night along the way or back?  Details:_____

Notes for next time (shuttles, entrance fees, parking, routes, etc):_____

# NOTES / JOURNALING

# FOURTEENER LOGBOOK

**DATE:** ☼ ⛅ ☁ ☁ ⛈ ❄ 🌬 ☐Hot ☐Cold ☐Mild

Start Date/Time:⠀⠀⠀⠀⠀⠀⠀⠀⠀⠀ End Date/Time:

Total Hike Time To Summit:⠀⠀⠀⠀ Total Distance Hiked:

Start Elevation:⠀⠀⠀⠀⠀⠀⠀⠀⠀⠀⠀ End Elevation:

Total Elevation Conquered:⠀⠀⠀⠀ Did you Summit on Day 1?⠀Y / N

**THE PEAK:** ☆ ☆ ☆ ☆ ☆

Peak Name:

Range:⠀⠀⠀⠀⠀⠀⠀⠀⠀⠀⠀⠀⠀⠀ Elevation:

Lat/Lon:

City, State:

Peak Conditions:

Cell Phone Reception/Carrier:

☐First Visit⠀⠀☐Return Visit⠀⠀Personal Rating: Easy / Intermediate / Difficult

14er Companions:

Route Taken:

Trail Features & Conditions:

Were there places to refill water?  Explain:

Did you stay the night along the way or back?  Details:

Notes for next time (shuttles, entrance fees, parking, routes, etc):

# NOTES / JOURNALING

# FOURTEENER LOGBOOK

**DATE:** ☀ ⛅ ☁ ☁ 🌧 ⛈ ❄ 🌫 ☐Hot ☐Cold ☐Mild

Start Date/Time:_____ End Date/Time:_____

Total Hike Time To Summit:_____ Total Distance Hiked:_____

Start Elevation:_____ End Elevation:_____

Total Elevation Conquered:_____ Did you Summit on Day 1?  Y / N

## THE PEAK: ☆☆☆☆☆

Peak Name:_____

Range:_____ Elevation:_____

Lat/Lon:_____

City, State:_____

Peak Conditions:_____

Cell Phone Reception/Carrier:_____

☐First Visit  ☐Return Visit   Personal Rating:  Easy / Intermediate / Difficult

14er Companions:_____

Route Taken:_____

Trail Features & Conditions:_____

Were there places to refill water?  Explain:_____

Did you stay the night along the way or back?  Details:_____

Notes for next time (shuttles, entrance fees, parking, routes, etc):_____

# NOTES / JOURNALING

# FOURTEENER LOGBOOK

**DATE:** ☀ ⛅ ☁ ☔ ⛈ ❄ 🌫 ☐Hot ☐Cold ☐Mild

Start Date/Time: _____ End Date/Time: _____

Total Hike Time To Summit: _____ Total Distance Hiked: _____

Start Elevation: _____ End Elevation: _____

Total Elevation Conquered: _____ Did you Summit on Day 1?   Y / N

## THE PEAK: ☆ ☆ ☆ ☆ ☆

Peak Name: _____

Range: _____ Elevation: _____

Lat/Lon: _____

City, State: _____

Peak Conditions: _____

Cell Phone Reception/Carrier: _____

☐First Visit   ☐Return Visit     Personal Rating:  Easy / Intermediate / Difficult

14er Companions: _____

Route Taken: _____

Trail Features & Conditions: _____

Were there places to refill water?  Explain: _____

Did you stay the night along the way or back?  Details: _____

Notes for next time (shuttles, entrance fees, parking, routes, etc): ____

# NOTES / JOURNALING

# FOURTEENER LOGBOOK

**DATE:** ☀ ⛅ ☁ 🌧 ⛈ ❄ 🌬 ☐Hot ☐Cold ☐Mild

Start Date/Time: _____  End Date/Time: _____

Total Hike Time To Summit: _____  Total Distance Hiked: _____

Start Elevation: _____  End Elevation: _____

Total Elevation Conquered: _____  Did you Summit on Day 1?  Y / N

## THE PEAK:  ☆ ☆ ☆ ☆ ☆

Peak Name: _____

Range: _____  Elevation: _____

Lat/Lon: _____

City, State: _____

Peak Conditions: _____

Cell Phone Reception/Carrier: _____

☐First Visit  ☐Return Visit    Personal Rating:  Easy / Intermediate / Difficult

14er Companions: _____

Route Taken: _____

Trail Features & Conditions: _____

Were there places to refill water?  Explain: _____

Did you stay the night along the way or back?  Details: _____

Notes for next time (shuttles, entrance fees, parking, routes, etc): _____

# NOTES / JOURNALING

# FOURTEENER LOGBOOK

**DATE:** ☼ ⛅ ☁ 🌧 ⛈ ❄ 🌫 ☐Hot ☐Cold ☐Mild

| | |
|---|---|
| Start Date/Time: | End Date/Time: |
| Total Hike Time To Summit: | Total Distance Hiked: |
| Start Elevation: | End Elevation: |
| Total Elevation Conquered: | Did you Summit on Day 1?   Y / N |

## THE PEAK: ☆☆☆☆☆

Peak Name:

Range: _____ Elevation:

Lat/Lon:

City, State:

Peak Conditions:

Cell Phone Reception/Carrier:

☐First Visit   ☐Return Visit   Personal Rating: Easy / Intermediate / Difficult

14er Companions:

Route Taken:

Trail Features & Conditions:

Were there places to refill water?  Explain:

Did you stay the night along the way or back?  Details:

Notes for next time (shuttles, entrance fees, parking, routes, etc):

# NOTES / JOURNALING

# FOURTEENER LOGBOOK

**DATE:** ☼ ⛅ ☁ ☁ ⛆ ⛈ ❄ 🌫 ☐Hot ☐Cold ☐Mild

| | |
|---|---|
| Start Date/Time: | End Date/Time: |
| Total Hike Time To Summit: | Total Distance Hiked: |
| Start Elevation: | End Elevation: |
| Total Elevation Conquered: | Did you Summit on Day 1?   Y / N |

## THE PEAK: ☆☆☆☆☆

Peak Name:

Range: _____ Elevation:

Lat/Lon:

City, State:

Peak Conditions:

Cell Phone Reception/Carrier:

☐First Visit   ☐Return Visit   Personal Rating:  Easy / Intermediate / Difficult

14er Companions:

Route Taken:

Trail Features & Conditions:

Were there places to refill water?  Explain:

Did you stay the night along the way or back?  Details:

Notes for next time (shuttles, entrance fees, parking, routes, etc):

# NOTES / JOURNALING

# FOURTEENER LOGBOOK

**DATE:** ☀ ⛅ ☁ 🌧 ⛈ ❄ 🌫 □Hot □Cold □Mild

Start Date/Time:............................ End Date/Time:......................

Total Hike Time To Summit:.............. Total Distance Hiked:.............

Start Elevation:............................ End Elevation:......................

Total Elevation Conquered:............. Did you Summit on Day 1?   Y / N

**THE PEAK:** ☆☆☆☆☆

Peak Name:.................................................

Range:.............................. Elevation:......................

Lat/Lon:.................................................

City, State:.................................................

Peak Conditions:.................................................

Cell Phone Reception/Carrier:.................................................

□First Visit   □Return Visit     Personal Rating:  Easy / Intermediate / Difficult

14er Companions:.................................................

Route Taken:.................................................

Trail Features & Conditions:.................................................

Were there places to refill water?  Explain:.................................................

Did you stay the night along the way or back?  Details:.................................................

Notes for next time (shuttles, entrance fees, parking, routes, etc):.................................................

# NOTES / JOURNALING

# FOURTEENER LOGBOOK

**DATE:** ☼ ⛅ ☁ 🌂 🌧 ⛈ ❄ 🌫 ☐Hot ☐Cold ☐Mild

Start Date/Time:................................ End Date/Time:...........................

Total Hike Time To Summit:................. Total Distance Hiked:..................

Start Elevation:................................. End Elevation:...........................

Total Elevation Conquered:................. Did you Summit on Day 1?  Y / N

## THE PEAK: ☆☆☆☆☆

Peak Name:...........................................................

Range:...................................... Elevation:.........................

Lat/Lon:................................................................

City, State:...........................................................

Peak Conditions:...................................................

Cell Phone Reception/Carrier:................................

☐First Visit   ☐Return Visit    Personal Rating:  Easy / Intermediate / Difficult

14er Companions:..................................................

Route Taken:.........................................................

Trail Features & Conditions:..................................

Were there places to refill water?  Explain:..............

Did you stay the night along the way or back?  Details:..........

Notes for next time (shuttles, entrance fees, parking, routes, etc):..........

# NOTES / JOURNALING

# FOURTEENER LOGBOOK

**DATE:** ☀ ⛅ ☁ 🌧 ⛈ ❄ 🌬 ☐Hot ☐Cold ☐Mild

Start Date/Time: ................................ End Date/Time: ................................

Total Hike Time To Summit: ................ Total Distance Hiked: ........................

Start Elevation: ................................ End Elevation: ................................

Total Elevation Conquered: .................. Did you Summit on Day 1?   Y / N

## THE PEAK: ☆☆☆☆☆

Peak Name: ................................................................

Range: ............................................... Elevation: ..................

Lat/Lon: ................................................................

City, State: ................................................................

Peak Conditions: ................................................................

Cell Phone Reception/Carrier: ................................................

☐First Visit   ☐Return Visit     Personal Rating:  Easy / Intermediate / Difficult

14er Companions: ................................................................

Route Taken: ................................................................

Trail Features & Conditions: ................................................

Were there places to refill water?  Explain: ................................

Did you stay the night along the way or back?  Details: ....................

Notes for next time (shuttles, entrance fees, parking, routes, etc): ........

# NOTES / JOURNALING

Made in the USA
Middletown, DE
20 December 2018